A Somerset Cook Book

A SOMERSET COOK BOOK

Edited by
Eileen Cockerham, Daphne Criddle, Marian Greswell

Illustrated by
Tim Hayward

The Merlin Press

First published in 1985

Published for The British Red Cross Society,
Somerset Branch,
by The Merlin Press, Spaxton, Bridgwater, Somerset

© 1985 The British Red Cross Society
All rights reserved

ISBN 0 9508493 1 6

Designed and printed in Great Britain by
Acanthus Press Limited, Wellington, Somerset

FOREWORD

Cooking is a craft and our county of Somerset is renowned for its craftsmanship. This new book of recipes, mainly from West Somerset, therefore should achieve its two-fold purpose; to give us all fresh ideas for our menus and to raise money for the new Red Cross Centre building in Williton.

The contributors, who are all connected with the Somerset Branch of the Red Cross in one way or another, are themselves efficient and imaginative cooks and the recipes have been chosen for their Somerset origin or ingredients. We are exceedingly grateful to them for letting us into the secrets of their own special dishes.

Our very real thanks too to our publishers, the Merlin Press, and to Mr Tim Hayward who has done the delightful illustrations for us without a fee.

We are very pleased to have been asked to write the foreword to this excellent collection of Somerset recipes, and we wish all its readers good cooking and good eating.

Walter and Hermione Luttrell
Joint Patrons of Somerset Branch, B.R.C.S.

FIRST COURSES

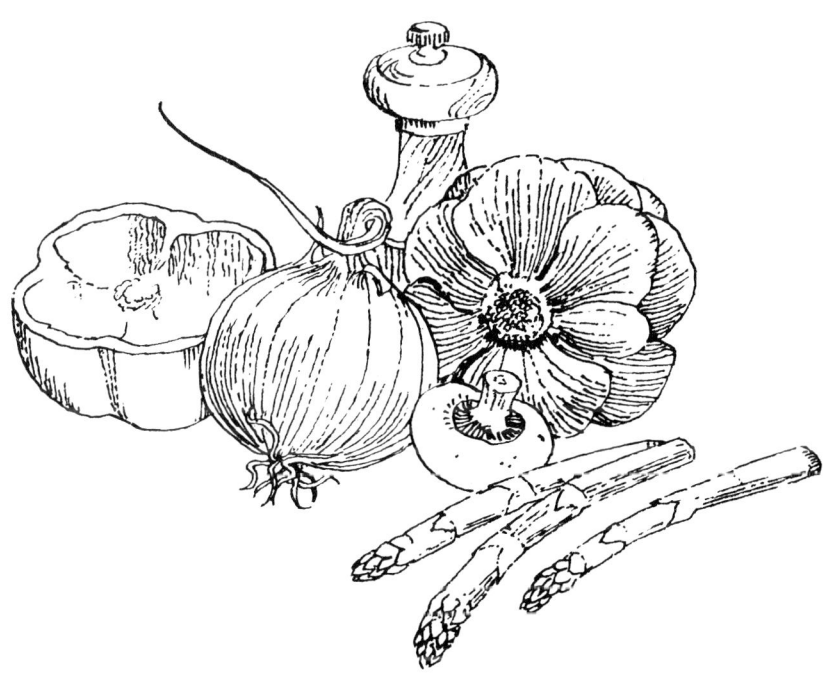

Brussels Sprout Soup

Serves six

900ml/1½ pints chicken stock
(or water and stock cubes)
450g/1lb fresh sprouts
(or 350g/12oz pkt frozen)
1 small onion
40g/1½oz margarine
40g/1½oz plain flour
500ml/1 pint milk
Salt and pepper
150ml/¼ pint single cream (optional)

Bring stock to the boil in a saucepan. Add prepared sprouts, bring back to boil and cover; simmer for 10 minutes. When cooked, liquidise in a blender. Meanwhile prepare and finely grate onion. Melt margarine in large saucepan. Add onion and cook slowly for 3 minutes. Gradually stir in the milk and bring to the boil, stirring. Simmer for 3 minutes. Add the vegetable purée and stir round. Season to taste. Serve with a thin trail of cream poured in bowl if desired.

Mrs Eileen Risdon

Spinach Soup

Serves four

Enough spinach to fill
 a large saucepan
25g/1oz butter
One potato (peeled and chopped)
One onion (peeled and chopped)
Stock
Salt and pepper
Nutmeg
Clotted cream

Wash and drain the spinach. Melt butter in saucepan, add the potato and onion, fry gently for 5 minutes, then add spinach. Toss in butter for a minute, then add stock to cover; simmer for approximately 30 minutes. Cool, then put in blender; add salt, pepper and nutmeg. Return to pan and reheat. Add a small teaspoon of clotted cream to each serving.

Mrs Alexander Payne

Withycombe Onion Soup

Serves four to six

450ml/1lb potatoes
900ml/2lb onions
50g/2oz butter
1 tbsp flour
300ml/½ pint milk

Peel and quarter potatoes and onions. Put in saucepan, just cover with water. Add butter and simmer for about 40 minutes or until vegetables have softened. Add milk and flour to thicken.
Pass through 'Mouli', using coarse grind, or mix very briefly in liquidiser. Keep hot until ready to serve.

Mrs Elizabeth Williams

Watercress and Potato Soup

Serves four

Butter for frying
1 medium onion — chopped
2 bunches watercress, washed and chopped
225g/½lb potatoes, peeled and diced
450ml/¾ pint milk
300ml/½ pint chicken stock
Seasoning

Melt the butter. Fry vegetables gently for five minutes. Stir in liquid, bring to the boil, add the seasoning. Lower heat and cool for 30 minutes approximately. Puree the soup and reheat.

Mrs Jean White

Geoffrey's Delight

Serves six to eight

1.8 litres/3 pints chicken stock
4 ripe avocado pears
Lemon juice
Salt and pepper
6 drops Tabasco
150ml/¼ pint double cream
Garnish:
Lemon slice
Whipped cream
Parsley or chives

Make sure stock is well flavoured and then chill thoroughly. Peel and halve avocado pears and remove stones. Brush pears generously on all sides with lemon juice as soon as you have cut and peeled them, to prevent them from discolouring. Purée avocado halves with chilled stock until smooth, in electric blender, or by rubbing through very fine sieve. Season to taste with salt and white pepper. Add Tabasco and cream; blend thoroughly; then taste again for seasoning, adding a little more salt or Tabasco if necessary, and lemon juice to taste. Garnish each portion with paper-thin lemon slice, topped with salted whipped cream and chopped parsley or chives.

Mrs Elizabeth Darke

Creamy Tomatoes

2 tomatoes per person
1-2 tbsps chopped walnuts
1-2 tbsps low fat cheese
2 tbsps walnut oil
1 tbsp wine vinegar
1 crushed clove garlic
150-300ml/¼-½ pint whipping cream
Salt
Freshly ground pepper
Chopped chives

Slice tomatoes thinly, and place in a dish with the chopped walnuts. Mix the remaining ingredients in a bowl and pour over the tomatoes. Chill before serving and garnish with the chopped chives.

Mrs Jean West

Avocado and Orange Starter

Serves four

2 ripe avocados
2 oranges
Lemon juice
Olive oil
Black pepper

Peel and slice the avocados and oranges and mix. Coat with oil and lemon juice, and sprinkle with freshly ground black pepper.

Mrs Anna Monico

Prawn and Pineapple Cocktail

Serves four to six

1 small fresh pineapple, or 1 large tin (without juice)
225g/8oz black grapes
450g/1lb peeled prawns
60ml/4 tbsp mayonnaise
30ml/2 tbsp whipping cream, lightly whipped
Salt and pepper

Peel pineapple and cut into small chunks. Mix pineapple, grapes, prawns and mayonnaise with cream. Season carefully to taste and serve on a bed of lettuce.

Miss Annabel Collier

White House Eggs

Per person:
1 cocotte dish (ramekin), or other small oven-proof dish
15g/½oz Stilton cheese
1 egg
1 tablespoon cream

Butter the cocotte dish and line with a thin layer of Stilton (grated or thinly-sliced), break an egg in it, season and place in a bain-marie or any covered pot containing about 2cm/1in of hot water. Bring to the boil, lower heat and simmer until the whites are opaque and set and the yolks still runny — this will take about 4-5 minutes but of course depends upon the size of the egg and also the type of dish used. Remove from bain-marie, add one tablespoon thick cream, grind on some more black pepper and a little sea salt, then sprinkle on the remaining Stilton. Place under a hot grill or in the top of a very hot oven for a few moments until the top is slightly brown and bubbling.

NB. If you find the Stilton cheese alone too tasty you may mix it with grated Cheddar — it will be delicious either way.

Serve as a hot starter or on its own for lunch, tea or supper.

Mr Dick Smith

Sheriff's Paté

Makes approximately 1¼lb

10 pigeon breasts
½ onion
1 tsp mixed herbs, pinches of basil and rosemary
15g/½oz streaky bacon
100g/4oz lard
100g/4oz butter
½ glass wine, sherry, port or whisky
Salt and freshly ground black pepper

Cut breasts from pigeons. Melt bacon and onion in fat in thick pan until cooked but not brown. Increase heat and sauté pigeon breasts. This should only take a few minutes and they should be pink inside. Add herbs, seasoning and wine to fat and let it bubble for a few seconds. Add to pigeon and liqudise, or mince very finely. Beat in sauce. Put into an earthenware dish or terrine and cover with melted butter. Chill and serve with hot toast.

Mrs Mary White

Stogumber Paté

Serves four to six

575g/1¼lb lamb's liver
6 tbsp port
Bay leaf and thyme
4 slices ham
350g/¾lb sausage meat
3 slices of bread soaked in milk

Marinade the liver in the port, with crushed bay leaf and pinch of thyme, for several hours. Mince the liver, ham, sausage meat and bread, mix well. Put in a tin, covered, and stand it in a container of boiling water in the oven, 180°C/360°F (Gas mark 4), for 1½ hours. Let cool in tin, with weights on.

Mrs Saville

Kipper Paté

Serves four

225g/8oz pkt kipper fillets
100g/4oz unsalted butter
Juice of ½ lemon
3 tbsp double cream
Pepper

Boil kippers, remove from packet. Place in shallow dish with lemon juice. Leave for half hour, combine all ingredients and liquidise. Chill well before serving.

Mrs Mary Randle

Curried Egg Mousse

Serves four

4 hard boiled eggs
1 tin Crosse and Blackwell's consomme
150ml/¼ pint double cream
2 dsp curry powder

Put all ingredients into liquidiser. Liquidise, and pour into dish. Leave in a cool place to set.

Mrs Rosemary Meadows

VEGETABLE DISHES

Herb Potatoes

675g/1½lb potatoes
25g/1oz butter
Mixed herbs
Salt and pepper

Line a shallow ovenproof dish with foil and grease lightly. Scrub potatoes and slice thickly. Place a layer of potatoes in the dish, dot with butter, sprinkle with herbs and seasoning. Add a further layer of potatoes, butter, herbs and seasoning. Cover tightly with foil and cook for about one hour at 190°C/375°F (Gas mark 5).

Mrs Jean White

Somerset Leeky Potato (High Tea or Supper Quickie)

Potatoes
Leeks
Margarine
Salt and pepper

Peel and thinly slice potatoes. Split white part of leeks lengthwise, cut into 1cm/½in strips. Wash thoroughly and drain. Melt small amount of margarine in heavy-based pan. Add potato, leeks, salt and pepper to taste. Stir to integrate. Cook on low heat 20-30 minutes. Stir occasionally. Serve piping hot. Makes a tasty accompaniment to omelette, cold meat or chicken.

Mrs Jenny Parfitt

Minehead Potato Casserole

Serves four

1.4kg/3lb potatoes
175g/6oz butter
3 medium tomatoes
1 large onion

Peel and slice the potatoes to approximately ½cm/¼in thickness. Place large knob of butter into frying pan and cook potato slices *gently* until opaque; do *not* brown. Grate onion and sprinkle between layers of potato in large casserole. Peel and halve tomatoes and place on top of last layer. Pour over any remaining butter. Cover with foil and cook at 190°C/375°F (Gas mark 5) for 1¼ hours approximately.

Mrs Jan Passmore

Baked Tomato and Marrow

Serves four to six

1 small marrow
4-5 tomatoes
25g/1oz butter

Peel marrow and remove pith and seeds. Dice into 2-3cm/1in cubes. Skin tomatoes by covering with boiling water and then skinning. Place a layer of cubed marrow in the bottom of a small casserole, cover with a layer of sliced tomato topped with a sprinkle of salt and freshly-ground black pepper. Fill the dish, finishing with a layer of tomato. Dot with butter and cook with the lid on for ½-¾ hour. This can be cooked in a hot oven with the joint, or in a cooler oven with a casserole or milk pudding, but the time will need to be lengthened if the oven is cooler.

Mrs Lesley Pring

Red Cabbage with Apple

1 small red cabbage
Salt
25g/1oz butter
1 onion
2 large cooking apples
Boiling water
3 tbsp vinegar
25g/1oz caster sugar

Remove outer leaves and cut cabbage into quarters. Cut away core and shred cabbage finely. Cover with cold salted water and soak for one hour. Melt butter in large saucepan. Peel and chop onions and fry gently for five minutes. Add red cabbage lifted straight from salted water. Peel, core and chop apples and add to pan; pour in sufficient boiling water to cover the base of the pan. Add vinegar and sugar. Cover, bring to boil and simmer for 45 minutes. Stir and press with potato masher occasionally to help pulp apples. Check seasoning and flavour.

For deep freezing: cool cabbage as quickly as possible, spoon into polythene bags, tie lightly and freeze.

To serve: while still frozen, place in a saucepan with 15g/½oz butter. Heat gently, breaking cabbage with a fork as it heats. Heat through until simmering. Serve with roast pork, duck or game.

Mrs Mary Jarman

Bean and Egg Au Gratin

Serves four

450g/1lb shelled broad beans
Salt
3 hard-boiled eggs, sliced
50g/2oz margarine
40g/1½oz wholewheat flour
450ml/¾ pint milk
Freshly-ground black pepper
2 tbsp fresh brown breadcrumbs
50g/2oz Cheddar cheese, grated

Cook the beans in salted water until just tender; drain. Place half the beans in a greased ovenproof dish and place the eggs on top. Cover with remaining beans. Melt 40g/1½oz of the margarine in a pan, stir in the flour and cook gently, stirring to make a roux. Remove from the heat and gradually add the milk, stirring. Return to the heat and bring to the boil. Cook, stirring until thickened. Season to taste with salt and pepper.
Pour sauce over the beans and sprinkle on the breadcrumbs and cheese. Dot with remaining margarine. Place in a preheated oven, 220°C/425°F (Gas mark 7), and cook for 15 minutes until golden brown. Serve immediately.

Mrs Julie Lepek

Cauliflower and Bacon Savoury

Serves four

1 large cauliflower
15g/½oz vegetable fat
1 onion
6 bacon rashers
For cheese sauce:
50g/2oz butter
40g/1½oz flour
450ml/¾ pint liquid
100g/4oz grated Cheddar cheese
Salt and pepper

Trim cauliflower and break into medium sprigs. Cook in boiling salted water until tender (about 10 minutes). Drain and reserve 150ml/¼ pint of cooking water for sauce. Arrange cauliflower sprigs in buttered dish and keep warm.
Peel and chop onion, and chop bacon rashers. Melt fat in frying pan, add onion and bacon and fry until onion is soft. Sprinkle over cauliflower and keep warm.
Melt butter in saucepan and add flour. Cook for about one minute, then add by degrees 300ml/½ pint milk and reserved cooking water. Cook for 2-3 minutes, then add cheese, salt and pepper; allow cheese to melt, then pour over cauliflower mixture. Sprinkle with a little cheese and pass under a hot grill until the top is crisp and brown.

Mrs Molly Jowett

Quantock Cauliflower

Serves four

1 very small cauliflower
100g/4oz carrots
1 tbsp cornflour
60ml/4 tbsp dry cider
300ml/½ pint stock
2 tsp tamari sauce
3 tbsp olive oil
1 large onion, thinly sliced
1 large clove garlic, finely chopped
100g/4oz cashew nut pieces
 (or sunflower seeds)
15g/½oz fresh ginger root, grated, or 1 tsp ground ginger

Chop cauliflower, keeping the fleurette shapes but making the pieces very small, 1-2cm (¼-¾in). Slice the carrots paper thin. Put cornflour in a bowl and gradually mix in the cider, stock and tamari. Heat oil in a large frying pan on a high heat. Put in the cauliflower, carrots, onion and garlic and stir them around on the heat until they begin to brown. Lower heat to moderate. Stir in the cornflour mixture and then the cashews and ginger. Cover the pan and keep on moderate heat for ten minutes.

Mrs Eileen Cockerham

Cashew and Tomato Loaf

Serves four to six

225g/8oz milled cashew nuts
225g/8oz fresh brown breadcrumbs
1 onion, finely chopped
200ml/⅓ pint tomato juice
25g/1oz oil
25g/1oz flour
1 tbsp chopped parsley
Seasoning to taste

Cook finely chopped onion in oil till tender. Add flour and the tomato juice and simmer, stirring, till it thickens. Stir in other ingredients. Place in a covered pudding basin and steam for ¾ hour. (Delicious with a tomato sauce or an onion Bisto gravy — served with roast potatoes and brussel sprouts.)

Mrs Elizabeth Saunders-Singer

Monks Pie

Serves two

450g/1lb potatoes
25g/1oz grated Cheddar cheese
2 eggs
Seasoning
Parsley

Boil and mash potatoes, put in bottom of greased pie dish. Make two holes in the mashed potatoes, sprinkle a little grated cheese into each hole. Rinse a small basin with cold water, break eggs into basin (water prevents sticking), then place in holes. Cover the top with salt and pepper, put a layer of grated cheese over the top. Put under hot grill until brown and crisp.

Mrs Jean Pulford

Lentil, Tomato and Mushroom Flan

Serves six

Shortcrust pastry:
175g/6oz plain wholewheat flour
Pinch of salt
75g/3oz vegetable margarine
2 tbsp cold water
Filling:
175g/6oz split red lentils
350ml/12 fl oz unsalted stock
 or water
1 large onion, peeled and chopped
25g/1oz butter
100g/4oz mushrooms,
 wiped and sliced
1 tbsp chopped parsley
100g/4oz grated Cheddar cheese
1 egg
Sea salt
Freshly-ground black pepper
2 tomatoes

Sift flour and salt into bowl. Using fingertips rub the fat into the flour until the mixture resembles breadcrumbs. Add the water and gently gather the pastry together into a ball, turn on to a floured board and roll out to required size.
Preheat oven to 220°C/425°F (Gas mark 7). Use the pastry to line a 20cm/8in flan dish, prick the base and bake the flan in the oven for about 15 minutes until it is set and crisp. Turn the oven down to 180°C/350°F (Gas mark 4). Wash and pick over the lentils, then put them into a saucepan with the stock or water and cook for 20-30 minutes, until liquid is absorbed. Fry the onion in the butter in medium-sized saucepan for 10 minutes. Stir in the cooked lentils, parsley, grated cheese, egg and plenty of seasoning. Spoon the mixture into the cooked flan case and smooth the top. Bake for about 40 minutes — watch it towards the end so that it doesn't become dry. (Delicious hot or cold.)

Mrs Margaret Dann

FISH

Baked Haddock

Serves four

4 haddock fillets
 (or less depending on size)
Celery soup
Breadcrumbs

Place haddock fillets in ovenproof dish. Pour over celery soup and cover with breadcrumbs. Bake in oven 200°C/400°F (Gas mark 6) for 15-20 minutes.
Miss Margaret Genge

Haddock and Mushroom

Serves four

100g/4oz mushrooms, sliced
25g/1oz butter
300ml/½ pint white sauce
½ tsp English mustard
25g/1oz grated Cheddar cheese
15g/½oz fresh breadcrumbs
225g/8oz smoked haddock, cooked, skin and bones removed, and flaked
Freshly ground black pepper
450g/1lb potatoes, boiled and mashed with 25g/1oz butter and 2 tbsp milk

Oven setting: 200°C/400°F (Gas mark 6). Melt butter in a pan, add mushrooms and sauté for about three minutes. Stir in white sauce, mustard, fish, and add pepper to taste. Choose a large dish or plate (a meat dish is suitable). Pipe a border of mashed potato round the edge. Pour mixture of mushroom and fish into the centre. Sprinkle with cheese and breadcrumbs. Dot with butter and cook for 15-20 minutes until topping is crisp and golden
Mrs Kay Jeffreys

Stuffed Mackerel

Serves one

1 mackerel
Few spring onions (chopped)
Parsley (chopped)
Pepper and salt
1 tsp lemon juice
25g/1oz softened butter
Breadcrumbs

Trim fish and make a pocket for stuffing in back of fish, if possible after the backbone has been removed. For the stuffing, mix all the ingredients together, using enough breadcrumbs to make a firm mixture. Spoon stuffing into pocket. Fry in hot oil to crisp up. Garnish with lemon slices.
Miss Margaret Genge

St. Audries Sole (or Plaice) with Orange

Serves four

4 sole (or plaice) skinned
Seasoned flour
50g/2oz butter
Chopped parsley
1 small orange, skinned and sliced
1 tsp sherry
½ tbsp tarragon vinegar

Cut off fins, wash and wipe fish. Coat them with seasoned flour and fry gently, one at a time, in 40g/1½oz butter, turning once to brown and cook each side. Keep warm. Combine orange slices and juice, sherry and vinegar and heat gently. When all fish are cooked, arrange on heated serving dish and keep hot. Clean pan and brown remaining butter lightly. Place orange slices down centre of fish, add liquid to browned butter and pour over fish. Serve at once, garnished with chopped parsley.

Mrs Kay Jeffreys

Tuna Mould

Serves four

200g/7oz tin tuna
225g/8oz cottage cheese
2 tsp gelatine
1 tsp horseradish
1 tsp sauce tartare
Squeeze of lemon juice
Cucumber, peppers, radishes, lettuce, watercress — to serve

Dissolve gelatine in a little hot water. When cool put with all other ingredients into a liquidiser. When well blended, pour into mould and leave in refrigerator to set. When required, turn out, garnish with cucumber slices, strips of peppers, radishes etc., and serve on a bed of lettuce and watercress.
This is a very versatile recipe. Slices on a lettuce leaf with suitable garnish make a very good starter; it can also be used as a sandwich spread with chopped cucumber.

Mrs Lucy Dearson

Herby Fish Mayonnaise

Serves five

900g/2lb cod or haddock
3 tbsp lemon juice
6 tbsp olive oil
3 tbsp mixed herbs: parsley, tarragon, chives, preferably fresh
300ml/½ pint mayonnaise
A little thin cream

Poach fish in small amount of water with one tablespoon of lemon juice and salt. Remove skin and bones and *while still hot* add oil, remaining lemon juice, herbs and salt and pepper. When cold spoon mayonnaise, thinned with cream, over fish. Garnish with prawns and parsley

Mrs Jean Gibbons

Somerset Smokie

Serves four

1 tbsp oil
175g/6oz lasagne
100g/4oz Cheddar cheese, grated
175g/6oz smoked, cooked haddock, boned and flaked
4 tbsp single cream
White sauce:
25g/1oz flour
25g/1oz butter
450ml/¾ pint milk

Cook lasagne in boiling, salted water with oil added for five minutes if fresh, or according to instructions on packet if dried. Drain well. Make white sauce, then add fish, half the cheese and cream. Layer lasagne and sauce in greased ovenproof dish and bake for 30 minutes at 190°C/375°F (Gas mark 6). Sprinkle with remaining cheese and return to oven for further ten minutes or brown under grill.

Mrs North

Sea Food Pancakes

Serves four (two per person)

1 packet Sainsbury's Batter Mix (or 300ml/½ pint home-made pancake batter)
4 scallops
2 small hake (or cod) cutlets
100g/4oz frozen prawns (defrosted)
150g/6oz mushrooms
50g/2oz butter
1 wineglass white wine
½ bay leaf
Salt
Black pepper
Squeeze lemon juice
300ml/½ pint thick white sauce

Lay scallops in pan and pour over white wine. Add pinch of salt and half bay leaf. Poach gently for 5-6 minutes. Draw aside. Put hake in foil with a little butter, salt, pepper and squeeze of lemon juice. Place in oven at 180°C/350°F (Gas mark 4) for 15 minutes until just cooked. Cook mushrooms slowly in butter for 3-4 minutes. Make half pint thick white sauce (must be thick because of the fish juices to be added). Add lightly chopped scallops, hake, fish liquor from both and the mushrooms and prawns. Season to taste. Keep hot.

Pancakes
Lightly cover small frying pan with oil and heat until smoking. Add one tablespoon pancake mix for each pancake, making them really thin. Stack between layers of greaseproof paper and place in oven to keep warm. Fill each pancake with generous helping of fish mixture. Serve piping hot with new potatoes and spinach.

Mrs Jane Denton

Spaxton Trout

Serves four

4 trout (gutted)
50g-75g/2oz-3oz butter
1 tbsp tarragon vinegar
2 tbsps chopped parsley
Salt and black pepper
Flour

Wash fish. Pat dry and roll in flour sprinkled with a little salt and pepper. Melt butter in frying pan, add the trout and fry until cooked and crisp on the outside. Remove trout to oven to keep warm. Add the tarragon vinegar to the remainder of butter in the pan, adding more butter if necessary. Chop the parsley finely, and stir into the melted butter. Pour over the fish and serve at once.

Mrs Jane Denton

Exmoor Salmon

Serves eight (generously)

800g/1¾lb salmon
Butter
110g/4oz button mushrooms (finely chopped)
½ onion (finely chopped)
75g/3oz butter
350g/12oz puff pastry
225g/8oz rice, cooked
2 tbsps chopped parsley
4 hard-boiled eggs, sliced
Salt and freshly ground pepper

Cut salmon into thin slices and sauté in butter until tender (or bake whole, wrapped in buttered paper and foil if preferred). Cool. Sauté mushrooms and onion in 75g/3oz butter until onion is transparent. Cool. Roll pastry into two rectangles, approximately 15cm x 20cm/6in x 8in; place one rectangle on greased baking sheet or large ovenproof dish. Combine rice with mushroom, onion and butter mixture; gently fold in salmon, hard-boiled egg and parsley. Place mixture on layer of pastry on baking sheet; season to taste with salt and pepper. Top with second rectangle of pastry, pinching pastry well together. Decorate with pastry leaves, brush with beaten egg and bake in a hot oven, 220°C/425°F (Gas mark 7) for 10 minutes, then reduce heat to 190°C/375°F (Gas mark 5) for about 20 minutes more. Serve hot.

Mrs Joan Northcote-Green

Cider-baked Mackerel

Serves two

2 fresh whole mackerel
Salt and pepper
Thinly-pared rind of half a lemon
1 onion, sliced into rings
275ml/½ pint dry cider
150ml/¼ pint water
1 tsp arrowroot
Thyme, rosemary (chopped)

Preheat oven to 180°C/350°F (Gas mark 4). Cut heads off the mackerel, clean and season inside of the fish with salt and pepper. Lay fish in an ovenproof dish. Add the lemon, onions and herbs. Pour over the liquids, cover with foil and bake for 30 minutes. When cooked, drain off 275ml/½ pint of liquid and reserve. Arrange the fish, onions and herbs on a dish and keep hot. Blend the arrowroot with a little water and stir into the reserved liquid. Pour into a saucepan. Bring to the boil stirring continuously. Simmer until the sauce goes clear. Pour over the fish and serve immediately.

Mr Steve Smith

Quick Salmon Dish

Serves two

1 small tin salmon
1 onion
1 tin sweetcorn
Butter

Fry onion until golden in butter. Stir in salmon and sweetcorn. Make a white sauce, add salt and pepper, and stir into salmon mixture. Serve with long grain rice or noodles. (Ten minutes to make.)

Mrs Pat Gurnett

MEAT, POULTRY & GAME

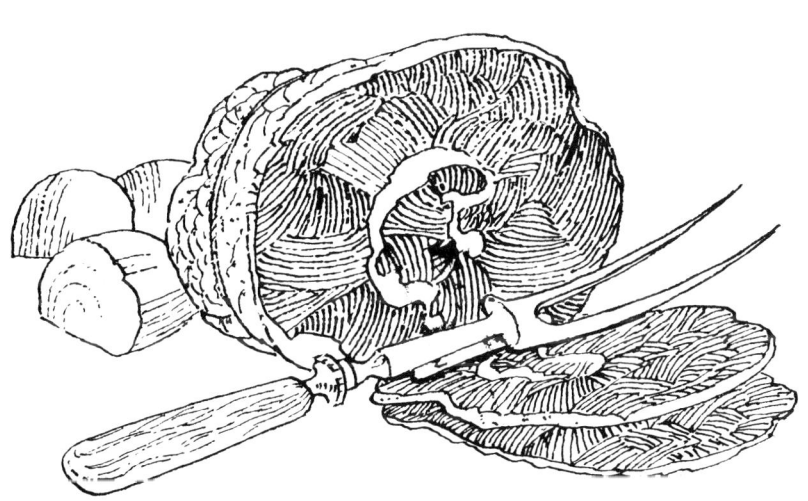

Somerset Pork Chops

Serves four

4 pork loin chops
25g/1oz butter
1 large onion, chopped
1 large apple, peeled, cored and chopped
300ml/½ pint cider
Salt and freshly-ground black pepper
100g/4oz double cream
Parsley for garnish

Fry chops in butter for five minutes each side, remove and place in a casserole. Fry onion and apple together for five minutes, add to chops. Pour over cider, season with salt and pepper. Cover and bake in oven at 180°C/350°F (Gas mark 5) for 45-60 minutes. Spoon over the cream and garnish with parsley sprigs.

Mrs Nanette Little

Pork Chops with Mushrooms and Cream

Serves four

4 large pork chops
175g/6oz mushrooms
1 tbsp plain flour
Seasoning
2 tbsp cooking oil
150ml/¼ pint single cream
Juice of one lemon

Trim the chops of fat and lightly fry each side in oil to seal and brown. Remove from pan. Place in baking tray lined with foil with sufficient overlap to envelop. Prepare and slice mushrooms, coat with flour and seasoning, and lightly fry. Divide mushroom mixture into four and place on the heart of each chop. Pour juice of lemon, followed by cream, over the chops. Fold over the tin foil, overlapping edges, and bake in a hot oven, 200°C/400°F (Gas mark 6) for approximately 1½ hours.

Mrs Rexworthy

Spicy Beef Stew

Serves five

900g/2lb stewing steak or shin
2 tbsp oil
1 large onion, chopped
1 tsp curry powder
½ tsp ground ginger
1 tsp sugar
1 tbsp Worcester sauce
Salt and pepper
450ml/¾ pint water
300ml/½ pint sour cream
2 tbsp horseradish cream
Chopped parsley

Cube meat and brown in oil in frying pan. Put in casserole with onion and all ingredients down to the water. Cook in a slow oven until tender. Stir in sour cream, horseradish and parsley, and if too thin add a little cornflour diluted with some of the cream. (If sour cream is unobtainable, use fresh with added lemon juice.)

Mrs Jean Gibbons

Boeuf Flamande

Serves three to four

450g/1lb braising beef
25g/1oz dripping
6 small onions
25g/1oz flour
Seasoning
Clove garlic
300ml/½ pint brown ale
300ml/½ pint brown stock
25g/1oz demerara sugar

Cut beef into large squares, colour in hot dripping, remove and colour onions golden brown. Drain off excess fat and stir in flour, add sugar, stock, beer and seasoning. Bring to boil. Put all into casserole and cook for about 1½ hours, until tender, at 180°C/350°F (Gas mark 3). Dish neatly and serve with creamed or duchesse potatoes.

Mrs Anne Luttrell

Lamb with Apricots

Serves four

675g/1½lb lean lamb, cubed
1 finely chopped onion
½ tsp ground cinnamon
¼ tsp ground ginger
225g/8oz dried apricots, soaked and liquidised or finely chopped
50g/2oz ground almonds

Simmer all ingredients for about two hours. Serve with plain boiled rice.

Mrs Anna Monico

Brendon Special

(A recipe devised during a camping holiday)

Serves four

2 tins stewing steak or 675g/1½lb steak and kidney, cubed
1 large onion
2 cloves garlic, peeled and crushed
100g-150g/4oz-6oz mushrooms, peeled and chopped
1 red pepper
4 large chopped tomatoes
½ bottle red wine or 300ml/½ pint dry cider
Mixed herbs
(Stock if using fresh meat)

Simmer all ingredients together until vegetables are tender (or for two hours if using fresh meat). Towards end of cooking time, add some tinned pineapple and juice. Serve with crusty bread, plain boiled rice or potatoes steamed over meat for last ¾ hour.

Mr Ken Almond

Liver Casserole

Serves four

225g/8oz liver
Seasoned flour for coating
30g/½oz butter
50g/2oz breadcrumbs
1 tsp mustard powder
2 small onions
300ml/½ pint stock
Herbs to sprinkle on top
Parsley to garnish
Dumplings:
100g/4oz self-raising flour
Pinch of salt
50g/2oz shredded suet
Cold water

Coat liver in seasoned flour. Lightly fry liver until browned slightly in butter on all sides. Mix the breadcrumbs with mustard powder. Prepare onions and lightly fry. Place a layer of liver in casserole dish, then a layer of onions, then a layer of breadcrumbs. Continue layers and end up with breadcrumbs on the top. Sprinkle with herbs. Place in oven at 180°C/350°F (Gas mark 5) for one hour. Mix suet, flour and salt, add water to make soft dough. Make into four balls. Place them on top of casserole 20 minutes before end of cooking time.

Mrs Brenda May

Two easy meals for one person

Breaded Liver

Lamb's liver
Olive oil or salad oil
Salt
Chopped rosemary
Breadcrumbs
Lemon juice
Double cream

Soak lamb's liver in oil for half an hour. Sprinkle each slice with salt and chopped rosemary, and coat with breadcrumbs. Grill for four minutes each side, sprinkle with lemon juice. If desired, serve with warm double cream to which a little lemon juice has been added.

Sautéed Kidneys

3 lamb's kidneys
100g/4oz mushrooms
1 onion
Cider
Butter
Parsley

Remove skin and core from kidneys and slice. Fry onion (chopped) in butter, until lightly browned. Add kidneys and stir. Blend in cider and add sliced mushrooms. Bring to boil then reduce heat and simmer gently for about 5-10 minutes until cooked. Stir in the chopped parsley. Serve with boiled rice.

Miss G. Genge

Cleeve Abbey Cheese and Ham

Serves six

1 medium onion, finely chopped
3 tbsp butter or margarine
3 tbsp plain flour
½ tsp dry mustard
175g/6oz Cheddar cheese, grated
325ml/12 fl oz milk
4 medium potatoes, sliced
350g/12oz cooked ham, diced
100g/4oz sliced celery
100g/4oz green pepper, chopped, *or*
100g/4oz tomatoes, chopped
Salt and pepper to taste

Sauté onion in melted butter or margarine until tender. Stir in flour, salt, pepper, mustard. Gradually add milk. Cook until sauce thickens and add cheese. Grease ovenproof dish and put alternate layers of potatoes, ham, celery, pepper or tomatoes and cheese sauce. Pour over remaining sauce and top with a little grated cheese and cayenne pepper. Bake at 180°C/350°F (Gas mark 4) for one hour with cover on, then remove cover and cook for further half hour. (To save fuel use cooked potatoes and reduce total cooking time to ¾ hour.)

Mrs Jeanne Webb

Savoury Sausage Snack

Serves one

2 sausages
Garlic salt or crushed garlic
Chopped mixed herbs
Cheddar cheese
Jacket potatoes or French bread

Grill or fry sausages until nearly cooked. Split almost through; sprinkle inside with garlic salt, or crushed garlic, and the chopped herbs. Insert thin wedges of Cheddar cheese into split and bake until cheese is melted. Serve very hot, with jacket potatoes or hot French bread.

Henry Greswell

Quick and Easy Supper Dish for one (or more)

For one

1 medium onion
2 rashers bacon
50g/2oz mushrooms
2 tomatoes
1 clove garlic (optional)
Piece of green pepper (optional)

Chop up small and fry in a saucepan, adding salt, pepper and herbs to taste. This makes a tasty sauce to go with any pasta or rice.

Mrs Jean Gibbons

Sausage and Potato Pie

Serves four

450g/1lb sausages
4 tomatoes
450g/1lb potatoes
1 onion
300ml/½ pint stock
Pepper and salt

Skin sausages and cut each in two or three pieces according to size. Peel and skin onion and potatoes. Slice tomatoes. Grease an oven dish and put in layers of potatoes, sausage and onion and tomato until all are used up, topping with a layer of potatoes. Season with pepper and salt as you fill the dish. Pour in the stock (or 300ml/½ pint water with half teaspoon meat extract added). Cover with lid or piece of greased paper and bake in moderate oven for one hour. Remove cover and bake for a few minutes more until brown on top. Serve very hot.

Mrs Wendy James

Picnic Pie

Serves four to six

450g/1lb puff or flaky pastry
450g/1lb minced steak
1 tbsp tomato ketchup
2 tsp Worcester sauce
50g/2oz rolled oats
1 large cooking apple, sliced
Salt and pepper
450ml/¾ pint stock
A little beaten egg
25cm/10in pie plate or dish

Fry mince, without extra fat; when brown, add ketchup, Worcester sauce and oats, salt and pepper. Stir in stock and bring to boil. Leave to cool. Cut pastry in half. Roll out one piece to line dish. Fill with cooled mixture, place sliced apple on top. Roll out remainder, place over dish, dampen edges and seal together. Trim, decorate with pastry scraps. Brush over with beaten egg. (Leave pie to rest for one hour if possible at this point, but this is not essential.) Bake at 220°C/425°F (Gas mark 7) for 25-30 minutes. Serve hot or cold. A popular pie for family picnics.

Mrs Marian Greswell

Eve's Chicken

Serves four

4 breasts of chicken
2 small tins Campbell's condensed celery soup
1 cup chopped celery
1 cup chopped walnuts
1 tbsp lemon juice
1 tbsp mayonnaise
2 sliced hard-boiled eggs

Cut up chicken and put all ingredients into a casserole dish. Cook in slow oven for 2-3 hours.

Miss Brenda Knight

Poulet Simla

Serves four

1 freshly roasted chicken
  (or chicken pieces)
½ pint stiffly whipped cream
1 tbsp of dry mustard
2 tbsp of Worcester sauce
Pepper and salt
Boiled rice
1 tsp dry curry powder
A little chopped chutney

Cut up and arrange the cooked chicken in a casserole. Add the mustard, Worcester sauce, pepper and salt to the stiffly whipped cream. Pour over the chicken and brown in the oven. Serve with the boiled rice flavoured with the curry powder and chopped chutney.
Mrs Rose Luttrell

Orchard Chicken

Serves six

6 pieces floured chicken
2 chopped onions
1 tsp coriander seed
¼ tsp ground cinnamon
¼ tsp powdered saffron
300ml/½ pint stock
450g/1lb sliced pears
225g/8oz sliced dessert apples
225g/8oz apricots
2 dsp ginger syrup
  (or honey and ground ginger)
Lemon juice
Salt and pepper to taste
Chopped parsley

Fry floured chicken and chopped onions. Add coriander seed, cinnamon, saffron and the stock. Simmer for 20 minutes. Add the sliced pears, sliced apples, apricots, ginger syrup, lemon juice, salt and pepper to taste. Cover and simmer till tender. Garnish with chopped parsley. A very useful dish when there is a glut of fruit!
Miss Helen Russell

Colonel's Nostalgia

Serves two

2 chicken breasts (or other pieces)
1 large onion
40g/1½oz butter
1 tbsp oil
2·tbsp cooking brandy
150ml/¼ pint double or
  whipping cream
1 tsp curry powder
Seasoning

Slice onions, sauté them in the oil and butter for 10 minutes in covered pan; stir occasionally. Add chicken, cover and cook for 30 minutes at gentle heat, turning occasionally. Stir in curry and seasoning and cook for five minutes. Add cream and brandy *off the heat*. Keep in low oven until ready to eat.
Dr Shirley Gover

Chicken in Cider

Serves four

4 chicken breasts
2 tbsp salad oil
25g/1oz butter
1 onion, chopped
2 level tbsp paprika
25g/1oz flour
150ml/¼ pint soured cream
150ml/¼ pint stock
150ml/¼ pint dry cider
5 tbsp sherry
1 level teaspoon tomato purée
Salt and pepper
175g/6oz small button mushrooms
Chopped parsley

Cook chicken in oil and butter to brown. Take out. Cook onion in oil and butter. Add paprika, flour. Cook. Add stock, sherry, cider, salt and pepper, and tomato purée. Bring to boil. Add chicken. Put into oven dish and cook slowly in oven for 30 minutes. Add soured cream and mushrooms, previously cooked in a little butter. Serve garnished with chopped parsley.

Mrs Hazel Hartley

Apricot Chicken

Serves four

4 chicken pieces
425g/15oz can apricot halves
40g/1½oz packet French onion soup
Set oven at 190°C/375°F
  (Gas mark 5)

Place a piece of foil in a roasting tin, large enough to enclose the chicken pieces. Wipe chicken and place in prepared tin. Pour over the apricots and syrup and sprinkle over the soup powder. Crimp foil edges to form a parcel. Bake in oven for 1 hour 50 minutes, open out foil and bake for further 20 minutes to brown. Arrange chicken and apricots on dish. Pour over all juices, garnish with parsley and serve.

Mrs Mary Field

Special Occasion Duckling

Serves two

1 roast duckling
1 tbsp duckling fat
1 tbsp plain flour
2 oranges
Lemon juice
300ml/½ pint duckling stock
1 tbsp brown sugar
Seasoning to taste

Peel outer skin from one orange, scraping off pith, and cut into thin strips. Boil in a little water until tender, add juice of both oranges and a little lemon juice. Add flour to duckling fat, heat to make a roux, then slowly add stock and juices. Stir constantly over a low heat, adding sugar and orange peel. Bring to boil, add seasoning and serve with the duckling which has been kept hot.

Mr Edward Hill

Partridge Perfection

Serves two

2 partridges
1 medium-sized cabbage, with good heart
175g/6oz streaky bacon
4 large carrots
175g/6oz pork chipolata sausages
Salt and pepper
A few juniper berries (if available)
2 cloves garlic, crushed
2 lumps of sugar
Grated nutmeg
1 tsp grated lemon rind
Stock

Brown partridges in bacon fat; blanch cabbage in boiling water for 7 minutes; drain carefully and cut into thin slices. Place a layer of cabbage at bottom of ovenproof casserole; on top place bacon rashers, carrots (whole), sausages and partridges. Season with salt, pepper, juniper berries, garlic, sugar, nutmeg and lemon rind. Cover with remaining cabbage, add stock to come about half-way up the mixture, cover and cook in a very slow oven, 150°C/325°F (Gas mark 2) for 4-5 hours.

Mrs Eileen Cockerham

Venison in Ale

Serves six to eight

2kg/4lb joint of venison, well hung, preferably from the haunch
225g/8oz brown sugar
2 tbsps black treacle
570ml/1 pint brown ale

Dissolve sugar and treacle in ale. Place venison in stewpan or casserole, cover with ale mixture, bring slowly to the boil. Simmer gently, with lid on, until tender (approximately 2½ hours). Serve with plenty of well seasoned mashed potato and swedes.

Pheasant Dish

Serves four

1 pheasant
75g/3oz raisins
3 4 cooking apples
1 tsp ground cinnamon
110g/4oz clotted cream
2 tbsps brandy
75g/3oz butter
Juice of half a lemon

Soak raisins for two hours. Slice apples and sauté lightly in butter. Place in ovenproof casserole. Drain raisins and place on top of apples. Brown pheasant in butter until brown all over. Place on top of apple-raisin mixture. In a small basin, mix cream, lemon juice, brandy and cinnamon; pour over pheasant, cover with lid and cook in moderate oven, 180°C/350°F (Gas mark 4) until pheasant is cooked (about 1-1½ hours). Carve pheasant and place on heated serving dish, with apple and raisin mixture around it.

Mrs Marian Greswell

Hill Farm Pheasant

Serves four

1 plump pheasant
75g/3oz butter
2 medium onions
2 carrots
3dl/½ pint dry cider (or white wine)
Bouquet garni
Stock
25g/1oz flour
Salt and black pepper
200g/½lb button mushrooms
200g/½lb pickling onions, glazed

Wipe pheasant and truss neatly. Heat 25g/1oz butter in a fireproof casserole, add pheasant and brown well all over. Peel and slice onions and carrots. Lift pheasant from pan and add onions and carrots to hot fat. Fry gently until slightly softened. Replace pheasant in casserole, add cider and bouquet garni. Cover and place in moderate oven, 190°C/375°F (Gas mark 5) and cook for one hour. Lift pheasant from pan, cool slightly and divide into serving portions. Strain cooking liquid and make up to 4½dl/¾ pint with hot stock. Return liquid to casserole. Blend 25g/1oz butter with flour to make a 'beurre manié'. Add in small pieces to hot liquid, stir until melted. Bring to boil, stirring until thickened and smooth. Adjust seasoning. Replace pheasant pieces in casserole. Quickly fry mushrooms and add with onions to contents of casserole. Reheat thoroughly, then sprinkle with chopped parsley and serve.

Mrs June Illingworth

PUDDINGS

Quarkhill Baked Apples

6 Cox's Orange Pippins
Brown sugar
Raisins
Cinnamon
Apple juice
Meringue topping:
2 egg whites
100g/4oz caster sugar

Core the apples and cut away part of the apple to make a hollow in the top. Put a teaspoonful of brown sugar into each apple and fill hole with raisins. Sprinkle cinnamon on to top of each apple. Place apples in ovenproof dish and pour enough apple juice into dish to cover bottom. For the topping, whisk egg whites until stiff then whisk in 50g/2oz sugar until stiff and shiny then fold in remaining 50g/2oz sugar. Place a spoonful of meringue on top of each apple to fill hollows. Cook for about 10 minutes at 180°C/350°F (Gas mark 4) until meringue is a pale golden colour, then reduce heat to 150°C/300°F (Gas mark 2) for about 40 minutes or until apples are soft and meringue is crisp.

Mrs Patricia Donner

Hot Apple Soufflé

Serves four

3 medium-sized cooking apples
Small piece lemon
1 tbsp sugar
2 egg whites

Peel apples and cook with the lemon. Sieve and add sugar. Cool. Beat whites of egg very stiffly and fold into purée. Put the mixture into soufflé dish and cook, 150°C/250°F (Gas mark 2) for ¾ hour. Serve with cream.

Mrs Alexandra Payne

Father's Garden Hat

Serves six

200g/8oz self-raising flour
100g/4oz chopped suet
50g/2oz sugar
Milk to mix
Approx. 200g/8oz cooking apples, weighed when peeled and cored
Cloves or ground cinnamon
Dark soft brown sugar

Mix flour, suet and sugar, add milk to mix soft dough. Divide mixture into two-thirds and one-third. Roll out larger portion and use to line a large greased pudding basin. Fill this tightly with sliced apples, sprinkled with brown sugar and whole cloves or cinnamon. Roll out remaining suet mixture, moisten edges with water, and use to cover pudding. Cover with greased paper (pleated), and steam for three hours. Turn on to large hot dish — if may collapse, but no one minds.

Mr John Greswell

High Church Pudding

Serves six

200g/8oz self-raising flour
 (or 100g/4oz self-raising flour
 and 100g/4oz breadcrumbs)
½ tsp salt
100g/4oz suet
50g/2oz sugar
1 egg
Milk to mix
Blackcurrant jam

Grease a medium pudding basin. Put two large tablespoons of jam in the bottom of the basin. Mix all dry ingredients, add beaten egg, two tablespoons jam and milk to mix to soft dropping consistency. Add to basin. Cover with greased paper, pleated to allow for expansion, and steam for at least two hours. Turn on to hot dish — a large one to allow melted jam to run down.

Mrs Rachel Greswell

Etheldreda's Lemon Pudding

Serves four to six

40g/1½oz butter or margarine
200g/7oz sugar
3 eggs
40g/1½oz flour
¼ cup lemon juice
1 tsp grated rind
1 cup milk

Heat oven 180°C/350°F (Gas mark 4). Cream butter, add sugar and cream together. Add beaten yolks and mix well. Stir in flour, lemon juice, grated rind and milk in order named. Beat egg whites with pinch of salt until stiff, not dry. Fold in. Turn into individual cups or large dish, set in pan of hot water and bake for approximately 35 minutes.

Mrs Marian Greswell

Baked Banana Weacombe

Serves four to five

Lay six peeled ripe bananas in a shallow fireproof dish, and sprinkle over them:
3 tbsp brown sugar
The juice of 1 lemon
3 tbsp water

Bake in a slow oven until the bananas are brown, adding half way through the cooking one sherry glass of rum. Serve with whipped cream, served separately.

Mrs Diana Fellowes

Wortleberry Pie

Serves six

400g/1lb wortleberries
150g/6oz sugar
(or less if fruit is very sweet)
4 tbsp flour
2 tsp semolina
1½ tbsp lemon juice
A little butter
200g/8oz quantity shortcrust pastry

Line a pie dish with three-quarters of the pastry. Pick over the 'worts' and combine them with sugar, flour, semolina and lemon juice. Pour mixture into pie dish. Dot with small pieces of butter, cover with a lattice of strips of the remaining pastry. Bake in a hot oven 230°C/450°F (Gas mark 8) for ten minutes, then reduce heat to 180°C/350°F (Gas mark 4) and bake until the crust is golden brown (about 40 minutes in all).

Mrs Joan Johnston

Rich Pastry for Mince Pies

Makes forty mince pies (900g/2lb jar of mincemeat)

350g/12oz margarine
175g/6oz soft brown sugar
1 egg
675g/1½lb self-raising flour

Cream together margarine and sugar. Add egg and then add the flour. Keep mixture warm. Cut in half to use.

Mrs Diana Bale

Almond Meringue

Serves eight

5 egg whites
200g/7oz caster sugar
150g/5½oz ground almonds
Vanilla essence
Chopped almonds
Icing sugar
Creme au beurre:
2 egg yolks
100g/4oz caster sugar
150ml/¼ pint milk
225g/8oz butter
100g/4oz melted plain chocolate

Grease and flour two Swiss roll tins. Whisk egg whites until stiff and fold in sugar, ground almonds and two to three drops essence. Spread mixture over tins and bake in centre of oven for 30-40 minutes at 180°C/375°F (Gas mark 4). While cakes are still hot, trim edges with a sharp knife, cut each cake in half lengthways and carefully remove to rack to cool. Make creme au beurre by creaming egg yolks with half the sugar until pale. Dissolve the remaining sugar in milk, bring to the boil and pour on yolks. Return mixture to pan and stir over gentle heat until it will coat the back of a spoon. Allow to cool. Cream butter until soft and add cooled custard gradually. Stir in melted chocolate. Sandwich meringue oblongs together with some of the creme. Spread top and sides with the rest, and press chopped almonds round the sides. Sprinkle icing sugar round edges and chill cake before serving.

Mrs Kay Jeffreys

Jan's Cheesecake

For base:
50g/2oz butter
100g/4oz digestive biscuits
25g/1oz brown sugar
For filling:
75g/3oz cream cheese
50g/2oz caster sugar
150ml/¼ pint double/single cream
Carton hazelnut yoghurt
15g/½oz gelatine

Melt butter and add crumbed biscuits and sugar. Spread over flan base or in serving dish and allow to set. Melt the gelatine in a little hot water and combine all the ingredients. Pour on to base and serve when cold and set. Decorate to taste.

Mrs Kay Jeffreys

Raspberry Walnut Torte

Serves nine to twelve (half amount serves four to five, but bake in 17cm-18cm/7in tin)

Base:
175g/6oz plain flour
50g/2oz icing sugar
100g/4oz butter
275g/10oz pack of frozen raspberries
50g/2oz chopped walnuts
Topping:
2 eggs
225g/8oz granulated sugar
100g/4oz self raising flour
1 tsp vanilla essence

Blend butter and sugar, add flour and press into base of 22cm/9in round pan. Bake at 180°C/350°F (Gas mark 4) for 15 minutes until light brown. Cool. (Base may be made in advance and stored.)
Drain 275g/10oz pack of frozen raspberries (or use fresh or bottled). Spoon fruit over base and sprinkle with approximately 50g/2oz chopped walnuts.
Topping: beat two eggs with 225g/8oz granulated sugar until fluffy. Add 100g/4oz self-raising flour and one teaspoon vanilla essence. Blend well and pour over fruit and nuts. Bake at 180°C/350°F (Gas mark 4) for 30-35 minutes, or until pale golden colour. Cool. Serve with sauce made from fruit juice thickened with cornflour. Equally good with blackcurrants.

Mrs Sybil Pearce

Edwardian Cream

600ml/1 pint milk
2 eggs
15g/½oz gelatine (1 pkt)
1 teacup caster sugar
A few drops of vanilla flavouring

Soak gelatine. Warm milk, take from heat and add beaten egg yolks, sugar and gelatine (a fairly large saucepan needed). Return to heat and bring to boil slowly. Remove from heat and add well-beaten whites of egg and flavouring. Pour into a mould to set.

Miss Marion Winn

Hazelnut Gateau

Serves eight

4 egg whites
225g/8oz caster sugar
100g/4oz ground hazelnuts
1 tsp white vinegar
300ml/½ pint double cream, whipped
225g/8oz raspberries
Icing sugar

Grease and line two 20cm/8in sandwich tins. Whisk egg whites until stiff, whisk in half the sugar, a spoonful at a time, until the meringue is glossy. Mix ground hazelnuts with the remaining sugar and fold into meringue with the vinegar. Divide the mixture between the tins, spread flat and bake in the lower part of the oven at 190°C/375°F (Gas mark 5) for 30 minutes. Turn off the heat and leave to cool in the oven. Remove, turn out and peel off the paper. Spread half the cream over one of the meringues. Arrange raspberries on the cream, reserving eight for decoration. Sandwich meringues together and dust with icing sugar. Pipe eight swirls of cream and decorate with raspberries.

Mrs North

Raspberry Mousse

Serves four

1 raspberry jelly
1 small tin Ideal milk
300ml/½ pint boiling water
75g/3oz frozen raspberries

Melt the jelly with the water. Stir until dissolved. Add the frozen raspberries and whisk until liquid is cool. Add the Ideal milk and whisk again. Pour into individual dishes and refrigerate for an hour. Before serving, cream or other decoration may be added.

Mrs Jean Hodge

Lemon Delight

1 lemon jelly
450ml/¾ pint milk
1 level tbsp granulated sugar
2 eggs

Make jelly up to 300ml/½ pint with boiling water. Make custard of egg yolks, sugar and milk. When cool, blend jelly and custard together. Fold in stiffly beaten egg whites. Best served from refrigerator.

Mr John Parfitt

Loganberry Soufflé

Serves six to eight

25g/1oz gelatine
4 tbsp water
75g/3oz caster sugar
900ml/1½ pints fruit purée, made from 675g/1½lb loganberries which have been liquidised and then sieved, using a plastic sieve and not a metal one (raspberries are also excellent)
3 egg whites
300ml/½ pint double cream
To decorate:
A few halved walnuts
Chopped walnuts

Prepare 1.25 litre/2 pint soufflé dish with a collar of greaseproof paper. Dissolve gelatine in water, add sugar and heat gently until dissolved. Fold in fruit purée and cool. When mixture has thickened slightly (just starting to gel), whisk egg whites and fold into purée with cream. Pour into soufflé dish and leave to set. Remove collar, coat edges with chopped nuts and decorate top with halved nuts. If using fresh fruit, decorate with whole fruit at the last moment.

Mrs Elizabeth Darke

Coffee Soufflé

Serves four

2 eggs
50g/2oz caster sugar
1 small tin Ideal evaporated milk
4 tbsp water
15g/½oz gelatine
1 tbsp Nescafé

Whip egg yolks and sugar until creamy and thick. Whip Ideal milk until thick. Add to egg and sugar. Melt gelatine and Nescafé in four tablespoons hot water. Stir into egg yolks etc. Whip egg whites till stiff and fold into the mixture. Top with whipped cream and decorate with grated plain chocolate. (Best eaten the same day and kept in cool place, but not in refrigerator.)

Mrs Hazel Hartley

Whisky and Ginger Cream

Serves four

2 tbsp whisky
2 tbsp ginger marmalade/preserve
2 tbsp caster sugar
Grated rind of one lemon
300ml/½ pint double cream
2 egg whites

Put whisky, marmalade, rind and sugar in bowl. Stir and leave for 15 minutes. Stir cream in slowly then beat with electric whisk until thick. Beat egg whites until stiff, then fold into cream mixture until well blended. Chill for 30 minutes.

Mrs Joan Northcote-Green

Lemon Cream

Serves six to eight

275g/10oz stale sponge cake*
2 large eggs
50g/2oz caster sugar
Grated rind of large lemon
1½ tbsp lemon juice
150g/5oz carton double cream

Line 15cm/6in tin with greaseproof paper. Grate cake into fine crumbs. Whisk together for five minutes egg yolks, sugar and rind. Add lemon juice to mixture. In another bowl whisk egg whites until stiff. In a third bowl beat cream until thick. Fold cream and whites into lemon mixture. Put crumbs and mixture into tin in layers. Freeze solid. Turn out.
* You can vary the taste of this by the cake crumbs used — chocolate gives a luxury taste and ginger intrigues people.

Mrs Celia Andrews

Castang Delight

Serves four

200ml/⅓ pint double cream
40g/1½oz meringues
1 tsp instant coffee
40g/1½oz burnt almonds
2 dsp Armagnac or brandy

Whip cream until stiff and add broken meringues. Stir the coffee powder into Armagnac or brandy and add to the cream and meringue mixture. Stir in the almonds but keep a few for decoration. Put mixture into a shallow dish or individual dishes. Decorate with almonds. Chill and serve.

Mrs Elizabeth Williams

Pineapple Surprise

2 pkts butter barmouth or digestive biscuits, crushed
50g/2oz melted butter
100g/4oz icing sugar
75g/3oz butter
2 eggs
1 can crushed pineapple
225g/8oz whipped cream

Add the melted butter to the crushed biscuits. Put three-quarters into the base of a fruit bowl. Beat the icing sugar, butter and eggs together until light and fluffy and pour on to biscuit base. Cover with drained crushed pineapple then whipped cream. Sprinkle rest of biscuit mixture on top and leave in fridge overnight.

Mrs Jean White

Refrigerator Pudding

Serves six to eight

175g/6oz sugar
175g/6oz soft butter
3 eggs
150ml/¼ pint double cream
2 tbsp coffee essence
Packet of trifle sponges
  or homemade sponge cake
Sherry or white wine
Chopped nuts

Beat butter and sugar until white. Add eggs, one at a time, beating thoroughly between each addition. Beat in coffee essence. Line the bottom of a soufflé dish or glass bowl with sponge cut in thin slices. Sprinkle with sherry or wine. Spread a layer of butter mixture evenly over the cake. Repeat layers until all is finished, ending up with a layer of cake. Refrigerate until needed (or freeze and defrost 12 hours before needed). Whip cream until thick and cover top. Sprinkle with chopped nuts. (This pudding can be made at least a week in advance, omitting the cream until the day of serving.)

Dr Winifred Kingsbury

Frozen Almond Cream

Serves four

300ml/½ pint double cream
2 egg whites
Salt
4 level tbsp caster sugar
100g/4oz almonds
  (blanched, chopped and toasted)
4 tbsp medium sherry

Whip cream till it holds shape. Whisk egg whites and pinch of salt till it holds a peak. Whisk in caster sugar one spoon at a time. Continue till stiff and glossy. Fold in whipped cream. Add almonds and sherry. Spoon into individual ramekin dishes and freeze. Decorate centre of each with chopped almonds before serving.

Mrs Hermione Luttrell

Strawberry Ice Cream

Serves at least six

225g/8oz strawberries
  (fresh or frozen)
175g/6oz sugar
2 egg whites
150ml/¼ pint cream

Liquidise strawberries (previously thaw if frozen). Pour into mixer bowl, add the sugar and egg whites, mix till stiff. Stir in the cream, well, with a spoon. Pour into a bowl and freeze.

Mrs Ista Stoddart

Furze Family Ice Cream

4 large eggs (separated)
300ml/½ pint whipping cream
100g/4oz caster sugar

Put egg whites in a large bowl and whisk until stiff. Add egg yolks to bowl and stir with a metal spoon, then lightly fold in whipped cream. Place in a container and put into freezer. Will take approximately six hours to freeze.
For *Blackcurrant Ice Cream*, add 4 tablespoons Ribena.
For *Tutti Fruiti*, mix 100g/4oz cherries, raisins, apricots and nuts and four tablespoons of rum or brandy together the day before. Also use double cream instead of whipping.

Mr Nigel Furze

Chocolate Bombe

Serves eight

450ml/¾ pint double cream
25g/1oz caster sugar
Grated chocolate for decoration
For the chocolate mousse filling:
175g/6oz plain chocolate
25g/1oz butter
6 egg yolks
6 egg whites

Use a 2 litre/3 pint domed pudding basin. Lightly whip cream with sugar. Spoon into basin and spread evenly to line basin. Put in freezer to set firm. Break chocolate into basin. Set over saucepan half filled with water. Add butter. Stir occasionally until melted. Add egg yolks, stir, take off heat. Stiffly beat egg whites and fold into chocolate. Pour into the cream-lined basin. Replace in freezer and leave overnight or longer until frozen hard. About two hours before serving unmould the bombe — dip basin into cold water up to the rim and then slip palette knife down sides. Turn out and leave in fridge 1-2 hours. Decorate with grated chocolate.

Mrs June Illingworth

Butterscotch Sauce

Hot for ice cream or sponge puddings

225g/½lb soft light brown sugar
50g/2oz butter
300ml/½ pint water
15g/½oz cornflour
Few drops of vanilla essence
Squeeze of lemon

Heat sugar and butter until sugar is melted and a good brown colour. Mix cornflour with a little water; add rest to the sugar. Boil for two minutes, add cornflour, essence and lemon. Stir until thick and clear.

Mrs Elizabeth Williams

CAKES & BISCUITS

Date and Walnut Sponge

100g/4oz margarine
2 tbsp syrup
300ml/½ pint milk
175g/6oz self-raising flour
50g/2oz ground rice or semolina
75g/3oz soft brown sugar
50g/2oz chopped dates
50g/2oz chopped walnuts
½ tsp bicarbonate of soda
½ tsp mixed spice
2 eggs

Melt fat, syrup and milk. Mix dry ingredients. Beat eggs. Add liquids (cooled) to dry ingredients, fold in beaten eggs. Put into two greased sandwich tins. Cook 30 minutes at 180°C/350°F (Gas mark 4). This makes two cakes, which can if required be iced with maple icing and decorated with walnuts.

Mrs Lucy Dearson

Bishop's Cake

225g/8oz flour
225g/8oz margarine
225g/8oz sugar
2 eggs
450g/1lb sultanas
100g/4oz peanuts (optional)
Grated rind of 1 lemon
225g/8oz marzipan paste

Cream margarine and sugar to a whiteish colour, add eggs one at a time and beat. Fold in sifted flour, then fruit, peanuts and grated lemon rind. Spoon half the mixture into a 20cm/8in cake tin, cover this with a rolled out circle of marzipan paste about ½cm/¼in thick and finally add the rest of the mixture. Cook in a moderate oven with a piece of brown paper on top (approximately 1¼ hours).

Mrs Margaret Clarke

Eggless Chocolate Cake

275g/10oz self-raising flour
½ level tsp salt
3 level tbsp cocoa powder
175g/6oz caster sugar
100g/4oz Trex
3 level tbsp golden syrup
300ml/½ pint milk
1 level tsp bicarbonate of soda
½ tsp vanilla essence
Chocolate frosting

Grease a 20cm/8in cake tin and line with greaseproof paper. Sift the flour, salt, cocoa and sugar into a bowl. Dissolve the bicarbonate of soda in a dessertspoonful of milk. Warm the milk, Trex and syrup together until liquid. Allow to cool. Add this to the dry ingredients together with the bicarbinate of soda and vanilla essence. Mix thoroughly. Pour into prepared tin and bake for one hour at 180°C/350°F (Gas mark 4). Cover and/or fill with chocolate cream frosting when cold.

Mrs Jill Sellick

The-Quickest-And-Best-Chocolate-Cake-In-The-World

225g/8oz granulated sugar
75g/3oz self-raising flour
40g/1½oz cocoa
Pinch salt
2 eggs
1-2 tsp milk
1 tsp vanilla essence
100g/4oz butter or margarine

Mix dry ingredients together, add eggs (beaten), vanilla essence and milk. Melt margarine (do *not* boil) and add when liquid. Bake at 190°C/375°F (Gas mark 5) for about 30 minutes. (Ice if desired.)
Mrs Janet Stocks

Ginger Cake

175g/6oz plain flour
75g/3oz sugar
75g/3oz butter and lard (mixed)
1 large tbsp golden syrup
1 large tbsp black treacle
1 tsp ground ginger
1 tsp mixed spice
½ tsp bicarbonate of soda
Pinch salt
1 egg and 150ml/¼ pint milk, mixed

Melt fats, sugar and syrups. Mix all dry ingredients. Add egg and milk to melted fats etc., then pour all into dry ingredients. Mix well, cook for one hour in medium oven 180°C/350°F (Gas mark 4). (This cake keeps well.) Especially good served with dessert apples on picnics.
Mrs Betsy Brigham

Churchwarden Cake

Put in saucepan:
175g/6oz margarine
1 cup brown sugar
1 cup water
450g/1lb mixed dried fruit
1 tsp bicarbonate of soda

Bring to boil, simmer for two minutes. Allow to cool. Add two eggs, 175g/6oz plain wholewheat flour and 1½ teaspoons baking powder. Pour into lined tin and bake 1¼-1½ hours at 160°C/325°F (Gas mark 3).
Mrs Hilary May

Bran Loaf

1 cup each:
Fine bran
Light brown sugar
Sultanas
Milk
1 egg

Mix all ingredients together, leave for one hour. Fold in 1½ cups of self-raising flour, put into lined loaf tin. Bake for 1-1¼ hours at 190°C/375°F (Gas mark 5). Turn down to 150°C/300°F (Gas mark 2) after 30 minutes. When cool, slice and spread with butter.
Miss Linda Criddle

Saturday Bun

2 cups self-raising flour
1½ cups mixed dried fruit
1 cup brown sugar
1 cup boiling water
100g/4oz margarine
1 tsp mixed spice
½ tsp ground ginger
1 pinch salt

Boil the water in a saucepan, add the sugar, margarine and fruit. Heat until the margarine has melted, then allow to cool a little and add the spices, flour and salt. Bake in a lined tin in a moderate oven for approximately one hour. (Can be eaten as a cake or, when baked in a loaf tin, cut in slices and buttered. Said to be a 'wartime recipe', it was introduced on picnics to the Acland-Hood family by relations in Ireland.)

Lady Gass

Banana and Nut Loaf

225g/8oz self-raising flour
50g/2oz butter
50g/2oz caster sugar
1 egg
50g/2oz chopped walnuts
75g/3oz golden syrup
2 bananas

Sift flour with a pinch of salt. Rub in butter, stir in sugar and chopped walnuts. Beat egg and blend with syrup and mashed bananas. Pour into dry ingredients and mix well. Turn into buttered loaf tin and bake for one hour at 180°C/350°F (Gas mark 4). Serve sliced and buttered.

Mrs Hermione Luttrell

Granary Loaf

To make a 900g/2lb loaf:
25g/1oz fresh yeast
½ tsp sugar
450ml/¾ pint hand hot water
675g/1½lb granary flour
1 tbsp sugar
1 tbsp salt
25g/1oz butter
Kibbled wheat flour for top

Dissolve yeast in a cupful of the measured water, put flour, sugar and salt into large bowl, rub in butter, then pour in yeast liquid and remaining water and mix to a dough. Knead for 5-10 minutes, put back in bowl, cover with cling film or a damp cloth and leave until mixture is double in size (about one hour in a warm place). Knock back, knead lightly and shape into a loaf and put in a greased bread tin. Cover again and leave for 30 minutes. Bake for 40-45 minutes at 220°C/425°F (Gas mark 7). Cool on a rack.

Mr Charlie Stevens

Lemon Satin Icing

50g/2oz margarine
2 large lemons or
4 tbsp pure lemon juice
675g/1½lb sifted icing sugar

Stir margarine and lemon juice in medium size pan over gentle heat until melted. Add 225g/8oz icing sugar and stir over low heat without simmering until sugar has almost dissolved. Cook for two minutes from time mixture begins to simmer gently at sides of pan until it boils all over surface. Remove from heat, stir in further 225g/8oz icing sugar, beat well with a wooden spoon. Pour into mixing bowl, beat well, scraping mixture from sides at intervals. Add remaining icing sugar, a tablespoonful at a time until icing is a soft doughy consistency. Turn mixture on to a board dusted with icing sugar and knead until smooth.

Mrs Kay Jeffreys

Chocolate Fudge Icing

Quantity for most sizes of cake, depending on thickness desired

75g/3oz butter or margarine
1 tbsp cocoa powder
1 tbsp warm water
200g/8oz icing sugar, sieved
25g/1oz walnut halves (optional)

Melt the butter or margarine in a pan. Blend the cocoa powder with the warm water and add to the butter or margarine. Remove from the heat and beat in the icing sugar. Leave to cool slightly and when thick spoon over the top of the cake. Make a swirled effect with a fork and decorate with walnut halves while the icing is still soft.

Mrs June Illingworth

St. Audries Sandwich

225g/8oz plain flour
50g/2oz lard
50g/2oz margarine
50g/2oz sugar
¼ tsp baking powder
Egg to bind
Lemon curd or jam for filling

Place dry ingredients in basin, rub in fats, add egg and turn on to floured board. Knead a little, cut in half. Roll out to line a sandwich tin, which has been well greased and lined with greased paper. Spread with curd or jam thinly, cover with other piece of pastry. Bake in moderate oven for 20-30 minutes.

Mrs Jean Pulford

Nut Fruit Slices

50g/2oz margarine
100g/4oz self-raising flour
1 egg
50g/2oz soft brown sugar
1 dsp syrup
100g/4oz dates
50g/2oz cherries
50g/2oz walnuts

Rub margarine into flour. Add chopped ingredients, then sugar, egg and syrup. Spread in a shallow tin, such as a Swiss roll tin. Cook 20-25 minutes in a moderate oven. Cut into squares when cold. (Water icing made with a little lemon juice can be drizzled on the top when cold.)
Mrs Daphne Underhill-Faithorne

Chocolate Fingers

225g/8oz butter or margarine
2 eggs
175g/6oz sugar
2 tbsp cocoa
3 tbsp self-raising flour
Vanilla essence
50g/2oz walnuts, chopped (optional)

Beat eggs, stir in sugar. Melt butter, add cocoa, mix well and add to eggs etc. Add flour (and chopped nuts if desired). Bake for 15 minutes in moderate oven 160°C-180°C/325°F-350°F (Gas mark 3-4) in a greased shallow tin.
Mrs Madge Anderson-Smith

Flapjack

175g/6oz margarine
75g-100g/3oz-4oz granulated sugar
1 dsp syrup
Combine:
250g/9oz porridge oats
½ tsp mixed spice
½ tsp cinnamon

Melt margarine, sugar and syrup until sugar is dissolved. Remove from heat and stir in oats, spice and cinnamon. Divide mixture between two greased 18cm/7in sandwich tins and press well down. Cook in oven 180°C/350°F (Gas mark 4) for ten minutes.
Mrs Gillian Tapp

Eric's Special Flourless Slices

175g/6oz cooking chocolate
50g/2oz margarine
100g/4oz caster sugar
1 egg
100g/4oz dessicated coconut
75g/3oz glacé cherries, chopped

Lightly grease a shallow tin (25cm x 15cm/10in x 6in). Melt chocolate. Pour into tin and cover base. Allow to cool and set. Cream margarine and sugar, beat in egg, stir in coconut and cherries. Spread mixture over the set chocolate and bake for 20 minutes at 180°C/350°F (Gas mark 4) until light brown. Leave until quite cold, then turn out and cut into fingers.
Mrs Lucy Dearson

Fridge Cake

75g/3oz butter
25g/1oz sugar
1 tbsp golden syrup
100g/4oz plain chocolate
225g/8oz digestive biscuits

Brush inside of 17cm-18cm/7in flan ring with a little butter and place on plate. Crush biscuits into crumbs using rolling pin. Melt chocolate, butter, sugar and syrup over a very low heat, add biscuit crumbs, stir well and pack into flan ring. (You can also add chopped nuts and cherries, but the Randle family prefer it plain.) Allow three hours to set. Store in fridge.

Mrs Mary Randle

Capton Slices

225g/8oz block chocolate
50g/2oz butter
100g/4oz demerara sugar
1 egg, beaten
50g/2oz mixed dried fruit
75g/3oz dessicated coconut
25g/1oz plain flour
50g/2oz glacé cherries, chopped

Line a small Swiss roll tin 28cm x 18cm/11in x 7½in with foil. Melt the chocolate and spread evenly over the foil. Leave to set. Cream the butter and sugar, beat in the egg. Add remaining ingredients, spoon into the tin and spread over the set chocolate. Bake in the centre of a cool oven 150°C/300°F (Gas mark 2) for 40 minutes until golden brown. Remove from oven, leave to cool for five minutes then carefully mark into squares with a sharp knife. Leave until cold, lift foil out of tin and peel away from chocolate. Finish cutting into squares with sharp knife.

Mrs Jean White

Bachelor Buttons

75g/3oz margarine
1 egg
75g/3oz sugar
150g/5oz self-raising flour

Cream margarine and sugar, add egg and flour. Taking small amounts the size of a walnut, roll in caster sugar, place on a greased baking sheet quite far apart. Bake at 200°C/400°F (Gas mark 6) for about 20 minutes. Cool on wire tray.

Mrs Sylvia England

Sticky Buds

175g/6oz Rice Krispies (one small packet)
100g/4oz margarine
100g/4oz soft toffees
100g/4oz marshmallows

Melt margarine, toffees and marshmallows in a saucepan on low heat. Stir a little, till marshmallows have dissolved completely. Turn off heat. Stir in gradually the Rice Krispies till every one is covered with the sticky mixture. Quickly put into a shallow tin such as a sponge tin (greased a little) and press down firmly, but not crushing the krispies. Leave to cool. This can then be cut into any shape you want. (Recipe given to Miss Tayler by an 11-year-old Guide.)

Miss Nancie Tayler

Krackolates

40g/1½oz (7 tbsp) Kellogg's cornflakes
20g/¾oz (1 level tbsp) cocoa
25g/1oz (1 tbsp) icing sugar
50g/2oz (1 tbsp) golden syrup
25g/1oz margarine
25g/1oz (1 tbsp) dessicated coconut
1 tsp grated orange rind

Melt margarine and syrup in saucepan. Do not boil. Add cocoa, remove from heat, stir in sugar. Using metal spoon fold in cornflakes, coconut and orange peel until coated. Spoon into cake cases. (Makes about 12 portions.)

Miss Virginia Nash

Mincemeat Slices

100g/4oz butter or margarine
225g/8oz self-raising flour
100g/4oz caster sugar
1 egg, beaten
3-4 tbsp milk to mix
Mincemeat
Brown sugar for topping

Grease a baking tray. Rub fat into flour until mixture resembles fine breadcrumbs and stir in the sugar. Make a well in the centre. Pour in the egg and enough milk to bind together. Turn the mixture on to a floured board, divide into two and roll out each piece to a 20cm/8in square. Lift one on to the baking tray, spread with mincemeat, place the other piece on top and press down firmly. Brush the top with milk and sprinkle with brown sugar. Bake just above the centre of the oven for about 20 minutes 190°C/375°F (Gas mark 5). When cold cut into 12 to 14 squares.

Mr Chris Hillier

Granola Bars

240g/8½oz instant porridge oats, toasted until pale brown
75g/3oz raisins
60g/2½oz chopped nuts
175g/6oz melted margarine
125g/4½oz brown sugar
150g/5oz honey
1 egg, beaten
½ tsp vanilla essence
½ tsp salt

Mix together all the ingredients. Press firmly into a well-greased Swiss roll tin. Bake for 20 minutes in oven 180°C/350°F (Gas mark 4). Cool and cut into bars. Store in a tightly covered container in the fridge. (Filling, chewy and not over-sweet.)

Mrs Eileen Risdon

Coleridge Cookies

225g/8oz margarine
1 tbsp water
2 tbsp syrup
2 large cups of oats
2 large cups of self-raising flour
1½ large cups of sugar
2 level tsp bicarbonate of soda
½ level tsp salt

Melt margarine with water and syrup. Mix dry ingredients and stir into cooled melted syrup mixture. Roll into small balls and place on greased and floured baking tins. Bake at 150°C-180°C/300°F-350°F (Gas mark 2-3) for 15 minutes. Leave to set for a minure or two before cooling on a rack.

Mrs Jill Killick

Sugar Crisp Biscuits

225g/8oz self-raising flour
225g/8oz caster sugar
100g/4oz butter
1 egg
½ tsp lemon juice

Rub butter into flour, add sugar. Knead with unbeaten egg and lemon juice. Roll out on floured board about ¼in thick. Cut into small rounds. Cook on greased baking sheet, leaving room to spread. Bake in moderate oven 150°C-160°C/300°F-325°F (Gas mark 2-3) until golden brown, 10-15 minutes.

Mrs Gwen Davidson

Tommies

75g/3oz ground hazelnuts
100g/4oz margarine or butter
65g/2½oz caster sugar
150g/5oz plain flour
Honey
Plain chocolate

Mix hazelnuts, margarine, sugar and flour. Drop in teaspoonfuls on a greased tray. Bake for 15 minutes. Cool and put together with honey. Ice with melted plain chocolate.

Miss Anna Ninnes

Petticoat Tails

175g/6oz butter
125g/4½oz icing sugar
250g/9oz plain flour
Approx. 1 tbsp cold water

Cream butter and sift in icing sugar. Beat in flour, adding sufficient water to make a firm dough. Roll out as thinly as possible, cut into triangles and bake at 170°C/325°F (Gas mark 3) for 20 minutes.

Mrs Peggy Cockroft

Chocolate Biscuits

Enjoyed by young and old

100g/4oz margarine
1 dsp sugar
2 dsp cocoa
2 dsp golden syrup
200g/½lb biscuits
2-3 squares cooking chocolate

Melt the ingredients in a saucepan over low heat. Do not boil. When melted and hot, stir in gradually ½lb crushed biscuits. Turn off heat. When evenly mixed put into a greased shallow tin 10cm x 28cm (about 4in x 11in) and press down hard with back of spoon. While doing this melt two or three squares of cooking chocolate and, before biscuit mixture cools, spread over with a knife. When cold cut into shapes.

Miss Nancie Tayler

Preserves, Cordials, Sweetmeats & Accompaniments

Spiced Pickled Plums

900g/2lb good plums
  (Victorias seem best)
300ml/½ pint vinegar
675/1½lb sugar
25g/1oz ground cinnamon
5g/¼oz allspice
5g/¼oz mixed spice

Wipe over plums, pack into jars. Boil together all other ingredients until mixture becomes syrupy. Allow to cool, pour over plums. Next day, strain syrup from plums, reboil to make it safe for keeping, cool again, pour over plums. When quite cold, cover closely and store for three months if at all possible. Serve with cold meats.
NB. After first day, when plums are strained they will feel soggy, but don't worry! They firm up when pickled and are very tasty.
Mrs Monica Bird

Spiced Pears

Makes about 1.75kg/4lb

1.75kg/4lb pears
  (dessert pears are best)
900g/2lb granulated sugar
600ml/1 pint malt vinegar
2 tsp whole cloves
2 tsp whole allspice
2-3 small pieces stick cinnamon
1 piece dried root ginger
2-3 pieces thinly pared lemon rind

Peel, core and quarter the pears. Place them in a bowl of water with a little lemon juice or salt to keep white. Lightly crush spices and crack ginger; tie loosely in a muslin bag and place in a large pan with sugar, vinegar and lemon rind. Bring slowly to the boil, add well-drained pears. Bring back to the boil and simmer for 15-20 minutes, or until pears are cooked. Lift out pears, drain well and pack into a wide-necked container. Return the pan of syrup to the heat and boil to reduce to about half; pour over pears to cover well. Cool and store ready for use in about one month.
Mrs G. M. Fisher

Runner Bean Chutney

900g/2lb runner beans
4-5 large onions
575g/1¼lb brown sugar
1½ tbsp turmeric
1½ tbsp mustard powder
1½ tbsp cornflour
900ml/1½ pints vinegar

Prepare beans and cook in salted water, also the onions. Strain both and chop up small. Add sugar and 750ml/1¼ pints of vinegar. Boil hard for 15 minutes. Mix turmeric, mustard and cornflour with the other 150ml/¼ pint vinegar and add to the mixture, and boil for a further 15 minutes. Allow to cool and put into jars. (Beans may be substituted with cauliflower and cucumber.)
Mrs Diana Salvidge

Red Tomato Chutney

3.5kg/8lb ripe tomatoes
450g/1lb onions
1 tsp dry mustard
900g/2lb white sugar (granulated)
4 cups white vinegar
2 tsp (level) salt
10g/½ carton pickling spice

Mince onions and peel tomatoes. Chop up. Add pickling spice in a muslin bag to all other ingredients except vinegar. Bring to the boil. Simmer until thick (this may take hours if tomatoes are juicy), and then add vinegar, and cook until a good consistency. The chutney may be thickened with cornflour, if necessary.

Mrs Diana Salvidge

Primrose Jelly

Put a quantity of primrose heads in a large pan. Add cooking apples, cut up but not peeled or cored (proportion should be one medium-sized apple to each large handful of primroses). Cover with cold water and boil until the apples are soft and pulpy. Put through a jelly bag and leave to drip overnight. Measure the juice and put it in a clean pan. To each 600ml/1 pint add 450g/1lb sugar and heat slowly until sugar is dissolved. Bring to the boil and cook until setting point is reached. Pour the jelly into hot jars and seal in the usual way. You may choose to add a few primrose petals just before the end of the cooking time — they look very pretty floating in the jelly.

Mrs Catharine Wilson

Elderflower Cordial

25 large elderflower heads
50g/2oz citric acid
1.5 litres/2½ pints cold boiled water
2 sliced lemons
1.4kg/3lb sugar

Put all ingredients into a bowl (NOT metal). Soak for two days, stirring whenever you pass by. Strain through muslin and bottle. (The cordial may be deep-frozen, provided open-top jars are used.) Drink diluted with water.

Mrs Ista Stoddart

Lemonade

Makes approximately five pints

6 lemons
1.75kg/4lb granulated sugar
50g/2oz tartaric acid
25g/1oz citric acid
50g/2oz Epsom salts
2.5 litres/4 pints boiling water

Grate rind finely into the granulated sugar. Add the acids and salts. Pour on the boiling water and stir until melted. Add lemon juice. Stir and bottle.

Miss Stella Maunders

Whiskey Wine

From a very old family cookery book

900g/2lb demerara or brown sugar
1 cup of wheat
6 old potatoes, cut up small or grated
450g/1lb raisins

Mix all together and cover with 12.5 litres/three gallons of boiling water, stir well and when mixture is just warm crumble as much yeast as will cover a penny (pre-metric 1d., approximately same size as 10p piece) on to a piece of toast, and add 10g/½oz of isinglass. Stir every day for three weeks, then take off all the scum, sieve well and bottle in stone bottles.

Miss Vera Yandle

Mulled Wine

Makes about 2.5l/4½ pints — two glasses each for ten people

900ml/1½ pints water
6 lemons, thinly sliced
12 cloves
   (can be inserted into an orange)
15cm/6in stick of cinnamon
1 tsp ground nutmeg
225g/8oz sugar
3 bottles red wine
   (home-made wine can well be used)
Slices of orange

Boil the water with spices and sugar, add lemons, stir well and leave for 15 minutes. Add red wine. Bring *almost* to the boil, but on no account allow to boil. Strain and serve in glasses decorated with orange slices.

Mr Geoffrey Darke

To Restore Voice

From an 1890 notebook

When the voice is lost from the effects of a cold, here is a simple remedy: Beat up the white of an egg; add to it the juice of a lemon and sugar to taste. Take a teaspoonful from time to time OR gargle the throat with warm olive oil every four hours (a few times will cure).

For a cough a baked lemon is an excellent remedy. Put it into a moderate oven and let it remain until soft. Mix together an equal quantity of honey and the juice of the baked lemon, and take a teaspoonful, which should be lukewarm, whenever the cough is troublesome.

For hoarseness — lemon juice squeezed on to soft sugar till like a syrup, and a few drops of glycerine added. Relieves at once.

Miss Stella Maunders

Fudge

Ideal to serve with after-dinner coffee

900g/2lb granulated sugar
225g/8oz butter
300ml/½ pint evaporated milk

Put all ingredients into a heavy saucepan over a low heat. Stir until sugar has dissolved, and bring to boil. Boil quickly until mixture reaches 115°C/240°F on sugar thermometer (soft ball stage) — about 10 minutes. Remove from heat and beat until thick (an electric hand whisk is ideal). Pour into greased tin 33cm x 22cm/13in x 9in and leave to cool, cutting into squares just before set. The fudge will keep for some time in an airtight tin.

Mrs Kay Smith

Mrs White's Famous Turkish Delight

25g/1oz gelatine
450g/1lb sugar
300ml/½ pint water
Essence of lemon flavouring
Cochineal to colour pink

Use two saucepans, and put sugar in one and gelatine in the other, and 150ml/¼ pint of water in each. The sugar must be brought to the boil but the gelatine just dissolved. Then mix both together in one saucepan and boil gently for 20 minutes, taking care not to let it boil over. Add flavouring to taste, and colouring. Put into *wet* dishes and allow to set overnight. Next day turn it out and cut into squares and roll in icing sugar to which a little flour has been added to prevent it from getting sticky. (Creme de menthe delight can be made by flavouring with essence of peppermint and colouring green.)

Mrs Gwynneth White

Chestnut Stuffing

100g/4oz breadcrumbs
50g/2oz suet
15g/½oz bacon, chopped
2 tsp chopped parsley
Grated rind of ½ lemon
¼ tsp mixed herbs
Salt and pepper
1 egg, beaten
A little sugar
450g/1lb chestnuts
300ml/½ pint stock
50g/2oz ham, chopped
25g/1oz butter, softened

Boil, skin and chop the chestnuts. Combine with all the other ingredients. Add extra breadcrumbs if consistency seems too moist.

Miss Jane Brodie

Dried Fruit Turkey Stuffing

1 large onion, finely chopped
225g/8oz prunes, soaked, stoned and chopped
225g/8oz dried apricots, soaked and chopped
2 cooking apples, peeled and chopped
1 tsp ground cinnamon
Butter

Fry the onion in butter. Add the chopped fruits and sauté for a few minutes. Stuff the turkey with the mixture.

Mrs Anna Monico

Old West Somerset Pudding

To serve with roast lamb — serves four to six

175g/6oz self-raising flour
50g/2oz shredded suet
1 small onion, finely chopped
2 tbsp mixed chopped herbs (fresh if possible)
Salt and pepper
Cold water

Place all ingredients in a bowl, mix to a soft dough with the cold water. Turn on to floured board, make into a round, flatten to about 5cm/2in thickness. Put in with the joint of lamb for the last hour of cooking so that it may take up some of the juices. Serve as one would serve Yorkshire pudding with beef. It should be light brown and crispish on the outside, soft inside.

Mrs Monica Bird

Cheese Dumplings

An appetising hot accompaniment to serve with sliced cold meat and salad — serves four

100g/4oz grated Cheddar cheese
2 eggs
Fat/oil for frying
50g/2oz margarine
225g/8oz white breadcrumbs
Pepper and salt

Cream margarine with grated cheese, and add lightly beaten eggs. Season to taste with salt and pepper and add enough breadcrumbs to make a stiff mixture. Form into dumplings and roll in breadcrumbs. Fry in hot fat or oil until brown and crisp.

Mrs Wendy James

Goose Pudding

100g/4oz scraps of bread
1 tbsp flour
Pinch of pepper and salt
Dripping (size of an egg)
1 tsp sage (rubbed down)
2 tbsp milk

Soak bread with boiling water and drain well; add dry ingredients and then add milk. Place mixture in well-greased tin; shred the dripping over the top and bake for 20 minutes. Cut in squares and serve hot or cold.
Miss Stella Maunders

Garlic Bread

2 medium cloves garlic
½ level tsp salt
100g/4oz butter
1 French loaf

Crush garlic with salt and beat into butter. Cut loaf in slices but do *not* separate them at the base. Spread both sides of each cut with garlic butter. Press together again and spread remaining butter on top and sides. Enclose in foil and bake in fairly hot oven 200°C/400°F (Gas mark 6) until hot right through and crisp.
Mrs Elizabeth Darke

Special Barbecue Sauce

1 large onion, chopped
1 stalk of celery (or celery salt)
1 tsp dried sage
150ml/¼ pint tomato purée
½ tsp salt
¼ tsp pepper
1 tsp dry mustard
1 tbsp demerara sugar
150ml/¼ pint red wine

Put all ingredients into pan. Stir till boiling, then simmer 15-20 minutes with lid on. Use with chicken, pork chops etc.
Mrs Windy Smith

And some tips for brighter breakfasts:

Ted's Marmalade

Take a dessertspoonful of marmalade from the jar, fill the 'hole' with whisky, or strong cider, replace the lid and watch the delighted faces around the breakfast table.
Mrs Monica Bird

Boiled Eggs

"I cannot even boil an egg . . . Oh yes I can, and what's more economise on gas or electricity."
There is no need to bring water to the boil BEFORE inserting the egg. Place the egg(s) in the saucepan, then cover it with cold water. Bring to the boil and switch off IMMEDIATELY. Leave the egg in the saucepan for three minutes (lightly boiled), four minutes (medium boiled), five minutes (hard boiled).
This method won a prize for two schoolboys in a BBC competition on 'How to save energy'.
Mr Roger Northcote-Green

Muesli

300ml/½ pint large flaked oats
150ml/¼ pint sunflower seeds
150ml/¼ pint sesame seeds
300ml/½ pint walnuts, chopped
300ml/½ pint coconut
300ml/½ pint margarine
300ml/½ pint honey
2 tbsp top of milk
1 tsp salt

Dry-fry sesame seeds in non-stick pan until brown. Melt margarine, honey, milk and salt. Mix into all other ingredients and bake in large roasting tin for one hour at 150°C/300°F (Gas mark 2). Stir frequently. After half an hour stir in 300ml/½ pint wheatgerm. Cool and store in airtight container. (This is a delicious breakfast with milk or fruit, and can also be used as a topping for crumble dishes.)
Mrs Elizabeth Williams

Index

Almond Meringue, 38
Apricot Chicken, 32
Avocado and Orange Starter, 10

Bachelor Buttons, 51
Baked Banana Weacombe, 37
Baked Haddock, 20
Baked Tomato and Marrow, 15
Banana and Nut Loaf, 48
Bean and Eggs au Gratin, 16
Bishop's Cake, 46
Boeuf Flamande, 27
Bran Loaf, 47
Breaded Liver, 28
Brendon Special, 27
Brussels Sprout Soup, 8
Butterscotch Sauce, 44

Capton Slices, 51
Cashew and Tomato Loaf, 17
Castang Delight, 42
Cauliflower and Bacon Savoury, 16
Cheese Dumplings, 60
Chestnut Stuffing, 59
Chicken in Cider, 32
Chocolate Biscuits, 54
Chocolate Bombe, 44
Chocolate Fingers, 50
Chocolate Fudge Icing, 49
Churchwarden Cake, 47
Cider-baked Mackerel, 24
Cleeve Abbey Cheese and Ham, 29
Coffee Soufflé, 41
Coleridge Cookies, 53
Colonel's Nostalgia, 31
Creamy Tomatoes, 9
Curried Egg Mousse, 12

Date and Walnut Sponge, 46
Dried Fruit Turkey Stuffing, 60

Edwardian Cream, 39
Eggless Chocolate Cake, 46
Elderflower Cordial, 57
Eric's Flourless Slices, 50
Etheldreda's Lemon Pudding, 37
Eve's Chicken, 30
Exmoor Salmon, 23

Father's Garden Hat, 36
Flapjack, 50
Fridge Cake, 51
Frozen Almond Cream, 43
Fudge, 59
Furze Family Ice Cream, 44

Garlic Bread, 61
Geoffrey's Delight, 9
Ginger Cake, 47
Goose Pudding, 61
Granary Loaf, 48
Granola Bars, 53

Haddock and Mushroom, 20
Hazelnut Gateau, 40
Herb Potatoes, 14
Herby Fish Mayonnaise, 21
High Church Pudding, 37
Hill Farm Pheasant, 34
Hot Apple Soufflé, 36

Jan's Cheesecake, 39

Kipper Paté, 11
Krackolates, 52

Lamb with Apricots, 27
Lemon Cream, 42
Lemon Delight, 40
Lemon Satin Icing, 49
Lemonade, 57
Lentil, Tomato and Mushroom Flan, 18
Liver Casserole, 28
Loganberry Soufflé, 41

Mincemeat Slices, 52
Minehead Potato Casserole, 14
Monk's Pie, 17
Mrs White's Famous Turkish Delight, 59
Muesli, 62
Mulled Wine, 58

Nut Fruit Slices, 50

Old West Somerset Pudding, 60
Orchard Chicken, 31

Partridge Perfection, 33
Petticoat Tails, 54
Pheasant Dish, 33
Picnic Pie, 30
Pineapple Surprise, 42
Pork Chops with Mushrooms
  and Cream, 26
Poulet Simla, 31
Prawn and Pineapple Cocktail, 10
Primrose Jelly, 57

Quantock Cauliflower, 17
Quarkhill Baked Apples, 36
Quick and Easy Supper Dish, 29
Quick Salmon Dish, 24
Quickest-And-Best-Chocolate-Cake-
  In-The-World, 47

Raspberry Mousse, 40
Raspberry Walnut Torte, 39
Red Cabbage with Apple, 15
Red Tomato Chutney, 57
Refrigerator Pudding, 43
Rich Pastry for Mince Pies, 38
Runner Bean Chutney, 56

St. Audries Sandwich, 49
St. Audries Sole (or Plaice), 21
Saturday Bun, 48
Sausage and Potato Pie, 30
Sautéed Kidneys, 28
Savoury Sausage Snack, 29

Seafood Pancakes, 22
Sheriff's Paté, 11
Somerset Leeky Potato, 14
Somerset Pork Chops, 26
Somerset Smokie, 22
Spaxton Trout, 23
Special Barbecue Sauce, 61
Special Occasion Duckling, 32
Spiced Pears, 56
Spiced Pickled Plums, 56
Spicy Beef Stew, 26
Spinach Soup, 8
Sticky Buds, 52
Stogumber Paté, 11
Strawberry Ice Cream, 43
Stuffed Mackerel, 20
Sugar Crisp Biscuits, 53

Tommies, 53
To restore voice . . ., 58
Tuna Mould, 21
Two Easy Meals for One Person, 28

Venison in Ale, 33

Watercress and Potato Soup, 9
Whiskey Wine, 58
Whisky and Ginger Cream, 41
White House Eggs, 10
Withycombe Onion Soup, 8
Wortleberry Pie, 38